Hello, America!

Liberty Bell

by R.J. Bailey

Bullfrog Books

Ideas for Parents and Teachers

Bullfrog Books let children practice reading informational text at the earliest reading levels. Repetition, familiar words, and photo labels support early readers.

Before Reading
- Discuss the cover photo. What does it tell them?
- Look at the picture glossary together. Read and discuss the words.

Read the Book
- "Walk" through the book and look at the photos. Let the child ask questions. Point out the photo labels.
- Read the book to the child, or have him or her read independently.

After Reading
- Prompt the child to think more. Ask: Have you ever seen the Liberty Bell? Did you see the crack?

Bullfrog Books are published by Jump!
5357 Penn Avenue South
Minneapolis, MN 55419
www.jumplibrary.com

Library of Congress Cataloging-in-Publication Data

Names: Bailey, R. J., author.
Title: Liberty Bell / by R.J. Bailey.
Description: Minneapolis, Minnesota: Jump!, Inc., [2016] | Series: Hello, America! | Includes index.
Audience: Grades K-3.
Identifiers: LCCN 2016009607 (print)
LCCN 2016010394 (ebook)
ISBN 9781620313497 (hard cover: alk. paper)
ISBN 9781624963964 (e-book)
Subjects: LCSH: Liberty Bell—Juvenile literature.
Philadelphia (Pa.)—Buildings, structures, etc.—Juvenile literature.
Classification: LCC F158.8.13 B37 2016 (print)
LCC F158.8.13 (ebook) | DDC 974.8/11—dc23
LC record available at http://lccn.loc.gov/2016009607

Editor: Kirsten Chang
Series Designer: Ellen Huber
Book Designer: Molly Ballanger
Photo Researcher: Kirsten Chang

Photo Credits: Adobe Stock, cover;
Alamy, 6–7, 8–9, 10, 11, 12–13, 16–17, 18, 23tl;
Corbis, 14–15, 23tr; Getty, 3, 20–21; iStock, 5;
Shutterstock, 1, 4, 19, 22, 23bl, 23br, 24.

Printed in the United States of America at Corporate Graphics in North Mankato, Minnesota.

Table of Contents

Let Freedom Ring!

We are in Philadelphia.
Wow! Look at the bell.

It has a big crack in it.

It is the Liberty Bell.

Sam tells us about it.

It is from 1752.

It hung in the center of town.

When it rang, people would gather.

Sam tells a story. The bell rang in 1776.

People came.
They heard
good news.

11

America had been part of England.

Now it was a free country!

People celebrated.

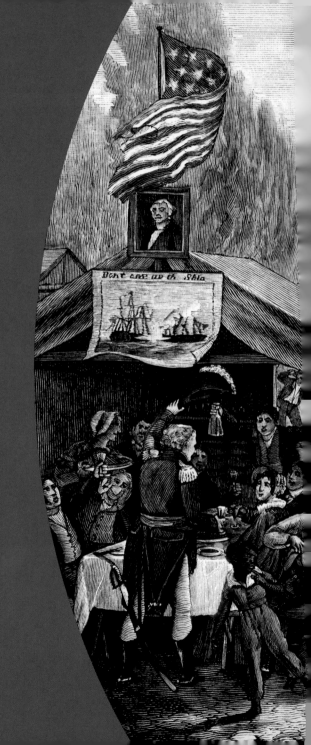

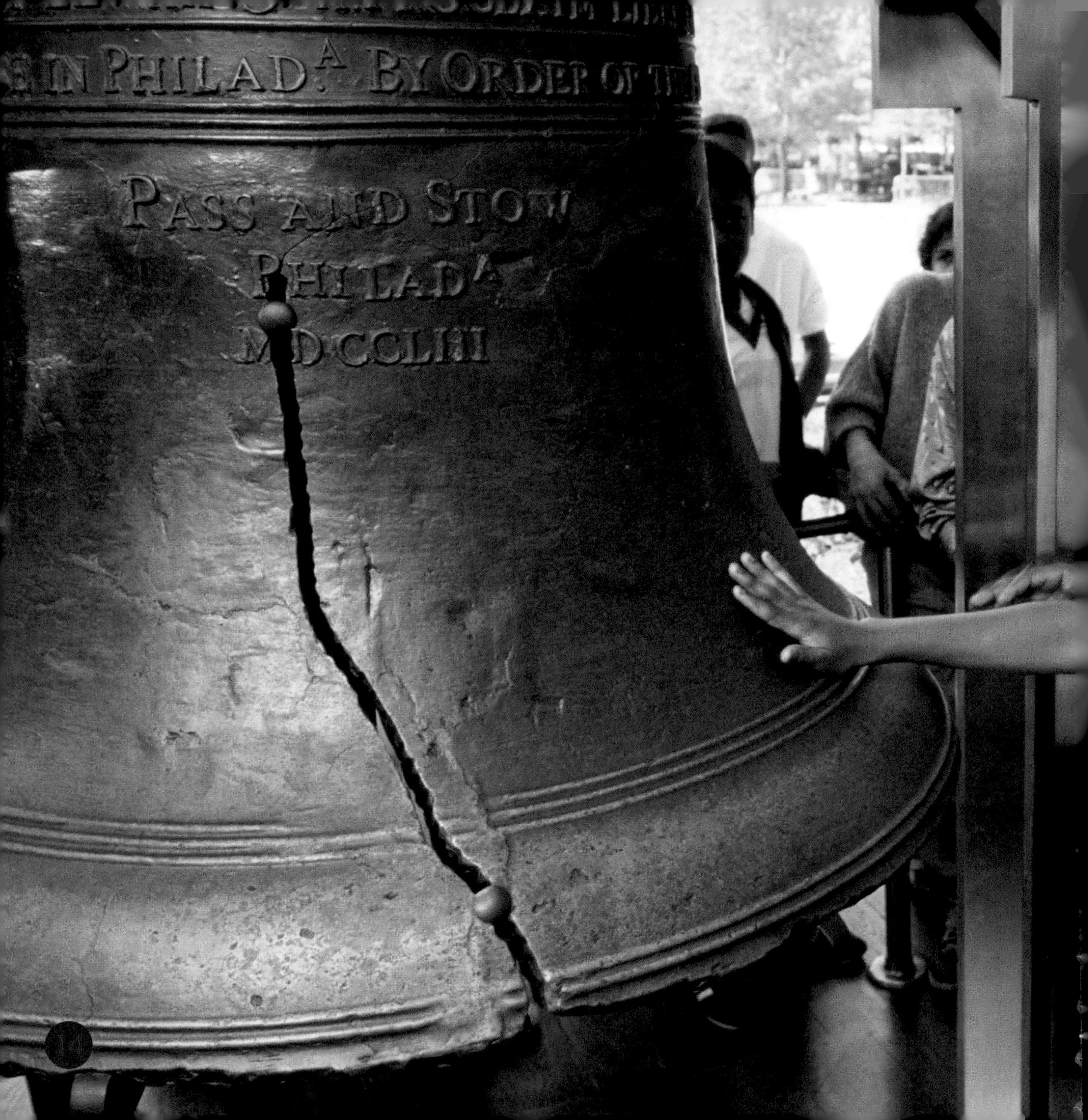
IN PHILADA BY ORDER OF THE
PASS AND STOW
PHILADA
MDCCLIII

We touch the bell.

What is it made of?

Metal.

It has words on it.

They say we are
all free.

M LIBERTY THRO
R OF THE ASSEMB

17

When did it get this big crack?

In 1846.

The bell rang. CRACK!
It did not ring again.

crack

The bell is quiet, but freedom rings!

Parts of the Liberty Bell

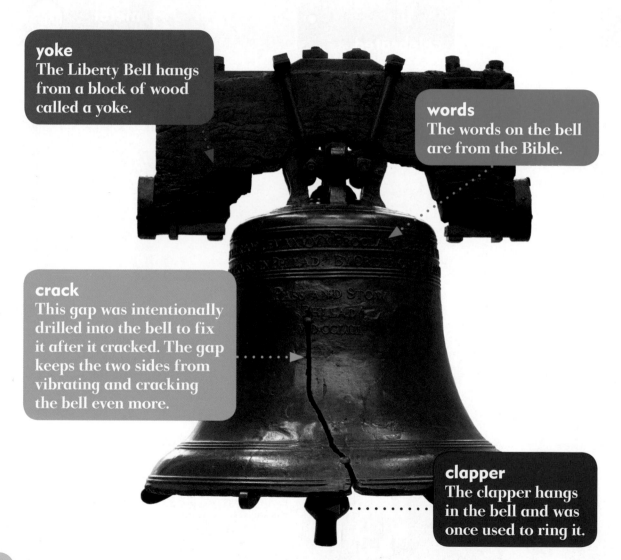

yoke
The Liberty Bell hangs from a block of wood called a yoke.

words
The words on the bell are from the Bible.

crack
This gap was intentionally drilled into the bell to fix it after it cracked. The gap keeps the two sides from vibrating and cracking the bell even more.

clapper
The clapper hangs in the bell and was once used to ring it.

Picture Glossary

celebrated
Observed in
a special way.

metal
A material, such
as gold, that is
shiny, conducts
heat, and can
be shaped.

England
A country in the
United Kingdom.

Philadelphia
A city in
the state of
Pennsylvania.

Index

To Learn More

Learning more is as easy as 1, 2, 3.

1) Go to www.factsurfer.com

2) Enter "LibertyBell" into the search box.

3) Click the "Surf" button to see a list of websites.

With factsurfer.com, finding more information is just a click away.